W9-ATT-080

THE
GREAT
BU$T
AHEAD

The Greatest Depression In American & UK History Is Just Several Short Years Away

This Is Your Concise Reference Guide To Understanding Why And How Best To Survive It

DANIEL A. ARNOLD

Published by Vorago-US

Copyright © 2002-2008
Daniel A. Arnold and Vorago-US

All rights reserved. No part of this book shall
be reproduced, stored in a retrieval system,
or transmitted by any means without written
permission from Vorago-US.
Please contact through the website below.

Published by Vorago-US
Fourth edition

Printed in the USA
20081

website:
www.thegreatbustahead.com

ISBN 1-59196-153-X

Jack –
sorry to be late
sending this. All the best. Jim

**Undoubtedly the gravest
warning of your lifetime**

Dedicated to my wife Linda

This book
is for the people of America
my home of thirty years

and

The people of the UK
land of my birth

Ideas, opinions and projections found in this book are strictly those of the author. They should not be acted upon without consulting with an independent advisor who is qualified to advise you on financial or investment matters. The circumstances of individuals vary widely, and must be very carefully considered. Readers are solely responsible for the consequences of any actions they choose to take based upon the contents of this book.

CONTENTS

Note: All charts in this book use linear scales. Vertical axis scales are not shown for demographic/DJIA values, as what is being displayed is solely for comparison of the shape of the two curves.

UPDATE, JULY 2007 - HAVE THIS BOOK'S PREDICTIONS PROVED ACCURATE?

When published in November 2002, prior to the Iraq war, oil price escalation and many of the major political and corporate scandals, this book predicted that:

1. The economy, as reflected by the DJIA, would resume its march upward following the controlling demographic starting in late 2002 or 2003 (pages 21,24). This is exactly what happened.

2. The DJIA would snap-back by 2004 to 13,000 to 14,000 and the FTSE in the UK to 6,000 to 7,000, but with a possible delay due to by terrorism, war, politics, and scandals. (pages 28,30). This is exactly what has happened. Although the full snap-back is still delayed for the reasons described, the DJIA has closed over 14,000 and the FTSE over 6,700.

3. The inflation-adjusted DJIA return from 2003 to 2012 would average 7% to 8% (pages 28,30). So far, with the effects of the delayed snap-back, the inflation-adjusted DJIA return has averaged less at about 6%, as would be expected.

4. Interest rates would increase from 2003 onwards (pages 47,48). This is exactly what has happened.

IMPORTANT UPDATE ON JAPAN

Firm data evidence now shows that Japan's thirteen-year severe recession from 1990-2003 was caused by a sustained decline in the "big-spenders" demographic group within Japan's population. This is the very same phenomenon that this book shows has controlled the American economy for the best part of a century, and that will also be the reason for the coming greatest depression in our history. See page 49 for the update. The fact that this same relationship can be found in the world's second largest fully industrialized democracy lends very powerful support to the thesis of this book.

INTRODUCTION

The entire purpose of this brief book is to warn and help prepare the average person, family, business and institution for the greatest economic event of our lives that is now steadily closing in on us. It is a once in a lifetime event, so there is little national memory that such an event is possible. It is the economic one hundred year flood. We are now just several years away from the greatest depression in American history. It will be several times greater than the 1930s. No maybe or perhaps. It is as unavoidable as it is certain.

The catastrophic events forecast with such clarity and certainty in the pages that follow are derived almost entirely from data that is in publicly available government files ranging from the Bureau of Labor Statistics to the CIA and the INS. Anyone with the very extensive time required, the inclination and good computer database skills can establish for themselves the veracity of everything presented in this book. The ideas and data presented are simple to understand. No degree in economics is needed here. The underlying concepts that lead methodically and relentlessly to the shocking results are so compelling that they are, to all intents and purposes, unchallengeable. If this seems an outrageous claim, you won't think so by the end of this brief and to the point book.

The book is intentionally brief to remain focused firmly on the core issue of the coming catastrophic depression. This way it is easily read without the unnecessary distraction of related topics, and quickly referred to as needed by the reader.

You will be shown that the fundamental long-term trend of the economy has almost nothing whatever to do with what you hear about all the time, such as interest rates, inflation, budget deficits, the dollar or who is in the White House or who controls Congress. Perhaps you have noticed these realities. A much, much more powerful, unstoppable force is the real trendsetter, and it is really so simple to understand. Every major economic event since 1920 will be easily and convincingly accounted for. It will seem so obvious once you've understood it, that what is forecast for the coming years will appear to be all but cast in stone . . . and in fact it is.

Chapter 1   THE EYE OPENER

After completing a two-year corporate General Electric Co. management training program, I worked for GE for a total of seventeen years in management and then consulting. I left GE to run full-time a small, growing manufacturing company that I had started a few years earlier in California. When the company was ten years old it was bought out by a larger company and I "retired" at the ripe old age of forty-four. I found myself with the challenge of seriously needing to understand investing. I continued to invest exclusively in mutual funds and soon went through some gut-wrenching and scary ups and downs, and losses. It didn't feel good at all. It was very clear to me that I did not have an adequate level of knowledge.

I embarked upon a search for the best wisdom of investing *long-term* in the American economy - i.e. the stock and bond markets. What I quickly discovered was simple and clear - no one had any idea of where the economy was going long-term. All the *constantly disagreeing analysts* were, and still are, focused on the short-term. Virtually no one tried to forecast the long-term. If anyone turned out in hindsight to have called something correctly, it seemed like pure luck. If you wait, even a useless broken clock is right twice a day! The summary of the best street wisdom on investing was and still is simply ***"Invest for the long-term (ironic don't you think), diversify and stay the course."*** Is this good advice? Sometimes good advice? Or is it perhaps now disastrous for the future?

In 1993 I came across a book entitled "The Great Boom Ahead" by Harry S. Dent Jr. (published by Hyperion). I felt intuitively that the concepts for forecasting the trend of the economy based on population demographics (how many of us, and the mix), made sense and were very interesting, even though the case was not proven. I may have found something close to what I was looking for, but not enough to bet the farm on - yet. I resolved to take the time and make the effort to create what was clearly a very extensive database, and use it to really test the ideas. Specifically I wanted to establish whether a piece of information in the book, that received very minor mention, was perhaps true. What was that piece of information?

One very simple sentence included the observation that *". . . . . the Mother of all Depressions would begin around 2010."* If this were true then it is the most important piece of information for everyone in the nation to know about, not the predicted boom times up to 2010 that the book dwells on, and that a follow-on book, "The Roaring 2000s" (published by Simon & Schuster), is devoted to. As you will see, "Roaring" is a substantial overstatement. What I found is something short of roaring, and what follows it is why this book is called **"The Great Bust Ahead."**

No one is meaningfully warning the general population of such a "bust" or depression. The two books mentioned give no details of it, do not quantify it or give a convincing account that it is in fact truly coming. This book does. Can you imagine what life will be like in the USA under such a scenario? What on earth will it be like for countries that depend so totally on the US economy, such as Mexico and Canada? The overall social and international consequences are truly scary. For the over 100 million baby-boomers (yes, it is really over 100 million, not the 75+ million you hear about - more on this later), it would certainly mean a very lousy retirement.

The public deserves to be warned clearly and convincingly about what is coming. The following chapters lead you methodically from the core underlying ideas through to the inescapable conclusion that a lengthy and catastrophic depression is soon to be upon us, and much of the rest of the world. As the saying goes, *"when America sneezes the world catches a cold."* If, a few short years from now, the USA contracts pneumonia, what on earth will the world contract?

Chapter 2   ECONOMICS 101
WITH A DIFFERENCE

It is a well-established and often quoted fact that 60-70% of the GDP (Gross Domestic Product - the sum of all goods and services the economy produces annually), is simply you and I spending. What we spend on food, vacations, cars, clothes and right down to a stick of gum is the greatest force in the GDP. This is why analysts say that if the consumer loses confidence and stops spending, the economy will go into recession. What makes up the rest of the GDP? Primarily it is the government (Federal + State) spending your money they take in as taxes (~28%) of all kinds. The two other main components are business investment (the buying of capital equipment and inventory), and the net of exports minus imports. In other words, you and I (directly, plus out taxes) are responsible for the overwhelming majority (90-95%) of the GDP. It is obvious isn't it? If none of us existed the GDP would be zero. It is the same in all industrialized democracies.

How could we test the truth of this *fact*? Well, if the GDP truly is primarily the simple consequence of our spending money, then the more of us there are the greater the GDP should be, right? Take a look at Chart 1. It is data compiled by the CIA on the GDPs of the fully industrialized democratic nations. It is

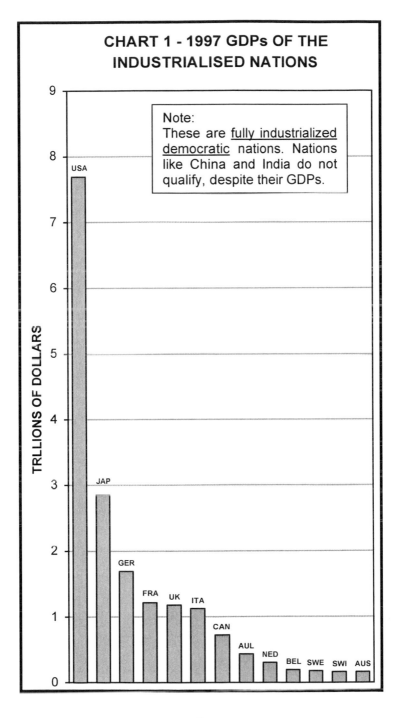

CHART 1 - 1997 GDPs OF THE INDUSTRIALISED NATIONS

Note:
These are fully industrialized democratic nations. Nations like China and India do not qualify, despite their GDPs.

TRLLIONS OF DOLLARS

USA
JAP
GER
FRA
UK
ITA
CAN
AUL
NED
BEL
SWE
SWI
AUS

expressed with a comparative concept called Purchasing (buying) Power Parity (PPP). Sure enough, the bigger the population the larger the GDP, with the USA way ahead of the pack. No surprise here. If "*we are the GDP*" is true, then dividing each country's GDP by its population should get very similar numbers for all countries. It does. Take a look at Chart 2. We are each responsible for about $22,000 of GDP. The variations between countries are mostly due to differences in productivity, with the USA leading the pack as expected, as we have the highest productivity. It is also interesting to note that the most productive industrialized nations seem to be the largest physically.

Now that we know that we *are* responsible for the GDP, it is only common sense that "who we are" *must* have a powerful bearing on the GDP. For example, if we were all fifteen years old with virtually nothing to spend, the GDP would be pathetic. If on the other hand we were all forty years old with good incomes (and spending it all as we do), the economy would be going gangbusters. *So, at any given time, the more of us with more money to spend there are, the better the economy (GDP) - obvious, but crucial to really understanding what drives the economy - as you will see.* Take a look at Chart 3. It is the Bureau of Labor Statistics data on how we spend with age.

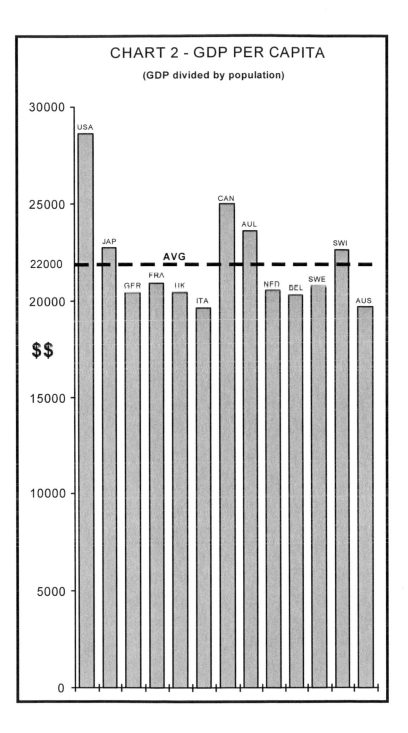

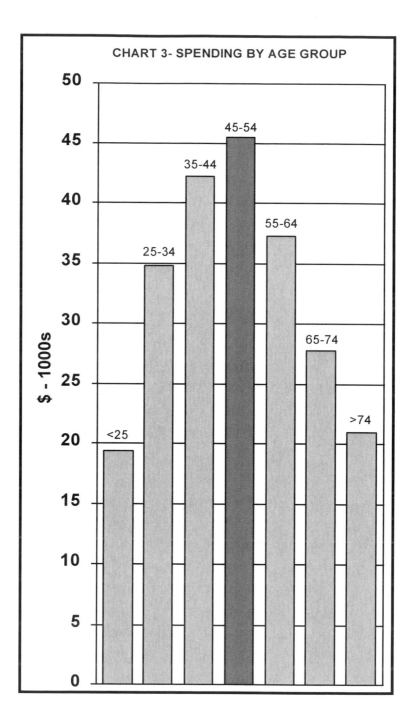

CHART 3- SPENDING BY AGE GROUP

The age group with the biggest spending is clearly the 45-54 years olds. This makes total sense of course. This is when our earned incomes are peaking, and our expenditures are greatest. We own our biggest house with its biggest mortgage and own our best cars. Our kids are in high school draining us dry, or are off to college at $10,000++ a year. Again, it is self-evident once pointed out.

In The Great Boom Ahead it is proposed that the ups and downs of the economy over time are caused by the ebb and flow of the number of these middle-aged big spenders in the population. Specifically, it focuses on the number of forty-nine year olds. A tantalizing correlation is shown between the number of 49ers and the trend of the economy, as expressed by the DJIA (Dow Jones Industrial Average). I wanted to rigorously test this for myself from the basic data, and improve upon the results if possible, in order to validate or invalidate the basic demographic concept once and for all. You see, it didn't make sense to me to focus on just one age of forty-nine. It seemed likely that the correlation would improve if a larger age grouping were used. After all, the government data of Chart 3 showed the peak spending was the 45 to 54 year old age group. This, not just one age within it, was clearly more likely to cumulatively have an effect on the economy, like a marching army. As you will see, I found that breathtaking results came when five-year age groupings were used. The age groups to use slowly changed towards the end of the twentieth century for another easy to understand, obvious reason that I will get to later.

How on earth do you find out how many people of a certain age are walking around in the population each year, for a hundred years or so period? Well, luckily the government keeps a record of all births. So if you want to know how many 50 year olds there were in 1980 just look up the number of births there were in 1930. Simple! Well, not quite. You see, the government only kept birth records starting in 1910. This only gets you the 50 year olds from 1960 onwards.

If you want to get a handle on 50 year olds from 1920 (my starting point) to 1959, you've got to go back as far as 1870 and find another source of births data. I chose to use US census data (taken every ten years 1860, 1870, 1880 etc.), and use the birth rate data they found per household. Using this, the birth rate per 1000 of the population and the size of the population, the number of births can be reliably estimated from the census data. The number of 50 year olds (or any other age) walking around each year from 1920 to 1959 was calculable with reasonable accuracy. This however is not the end of the story. The US has very substantial, and often huge, immigration just about all the time. Take a look at Chart 4. It shows INS legal immigration data from 1870 to 1998. Notice the massive immigration in the early 1900s and also the huge spike around 1990. (Remember both). Immigration data shows that the average age of immigrants is consistently about thirty. So, to get a better picture of how many 50 year olds there really were walking around in 1980 say, you would add part of the immigration number from 1960 to the births in 1930. For 1929 (now there's a date to think about), you would use birth estimates for 1879 added to part of the immigration from 1909. So, let's try plotting the 45 to 49 five-year age group against the DJIA for 1920 to 2001 and see what it looks like. Take a look at Chart 5. Well, there is not too much correlation there to hang your hat on. Oh, but we've forgotten one thing - inflation. To reflect its true value, let's adjust the DJIA for inflation using the annual CPI (consumer price index issued by the government). Now take a look at Chart 6. Not bad! However, something is clearly affecting things from about 1985 onwards. The demographic curve of 45-49 year olds is climbing very steeply (it's those baby-boomers!), but the DJIA (economy) isn't responding until several years later. Why?

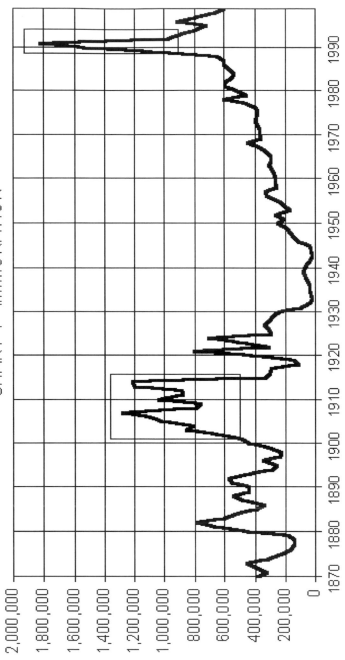

CHART 4 - IMMIGRATION

CHART 5 - DJIA vs DEMOGRAPHIC PROFILE

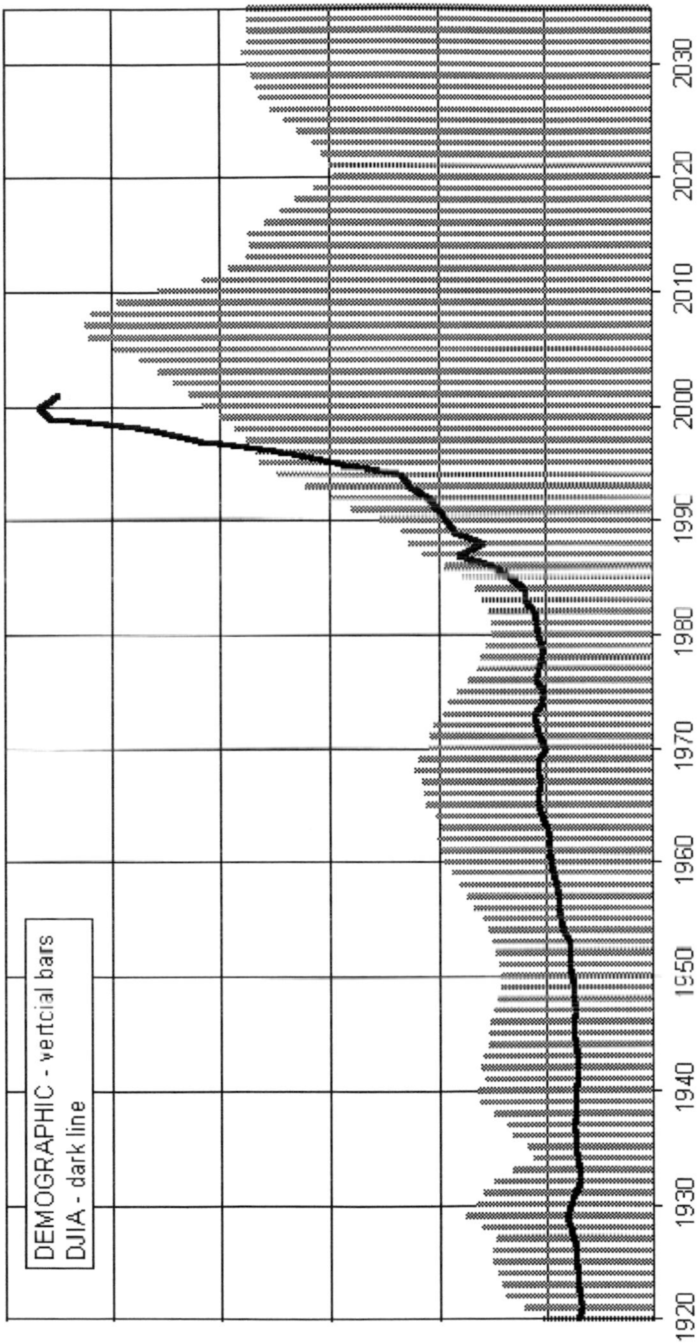

DEMOGRAPHIC - vertcial bars
DJIA - dark line

CHART 6 - INFLATION CORRECTED DJIA vs DEMOGRAPHIC PROFILE

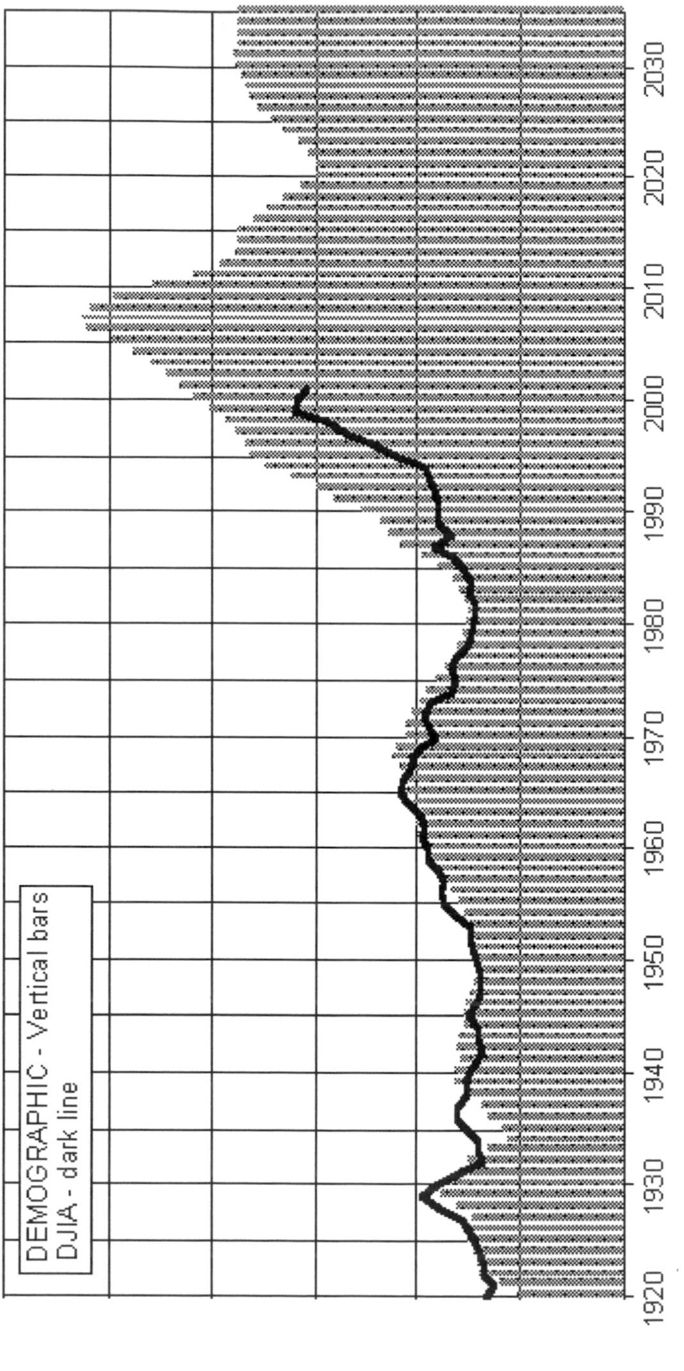

DEMOGRAPHIC - Vertical bars
DJIA - dark line

What could have happened to those who were 45 to 49 around 1985 that has pushed their high spending several years further into the future? You don't have to look far to find the obvious answer - the birth control pill. Introduced in the early sixties to women in their early twenties, it enabled more and more couples in the years following to push the start of their families out several years. This in turn pushed out their teenager, college, and bigger house expenditures etc. These "early baby-boomer women" (born around 1940), were in their early twenties in the early 1960s, **and in their mid to late forties in the mid 1980s**. So, in Chart 3 we now know why the high spending group goes out to age 54. We can begin to progressively move the demographic five-year group out to age 54 from the early 1980s onwards.

Let's plot this "pill corrected" demographic curve against the inflation-adjusted DJIA. Take a look at Chart 7. Much better, but the DJIA curve is clearly not now as high as it should be from 1990 onwards. Why? What else was at work stopping the DJIA rising as high as it should? Again, you don't have to look very far to find the answer - NASDAQ. In the 1990s the Nasdaq exploded, sucking money away from the traditional large cap stocks of the DJIA, and into (typically) technology stocks, in exactly the same way that money going into stocks draws money

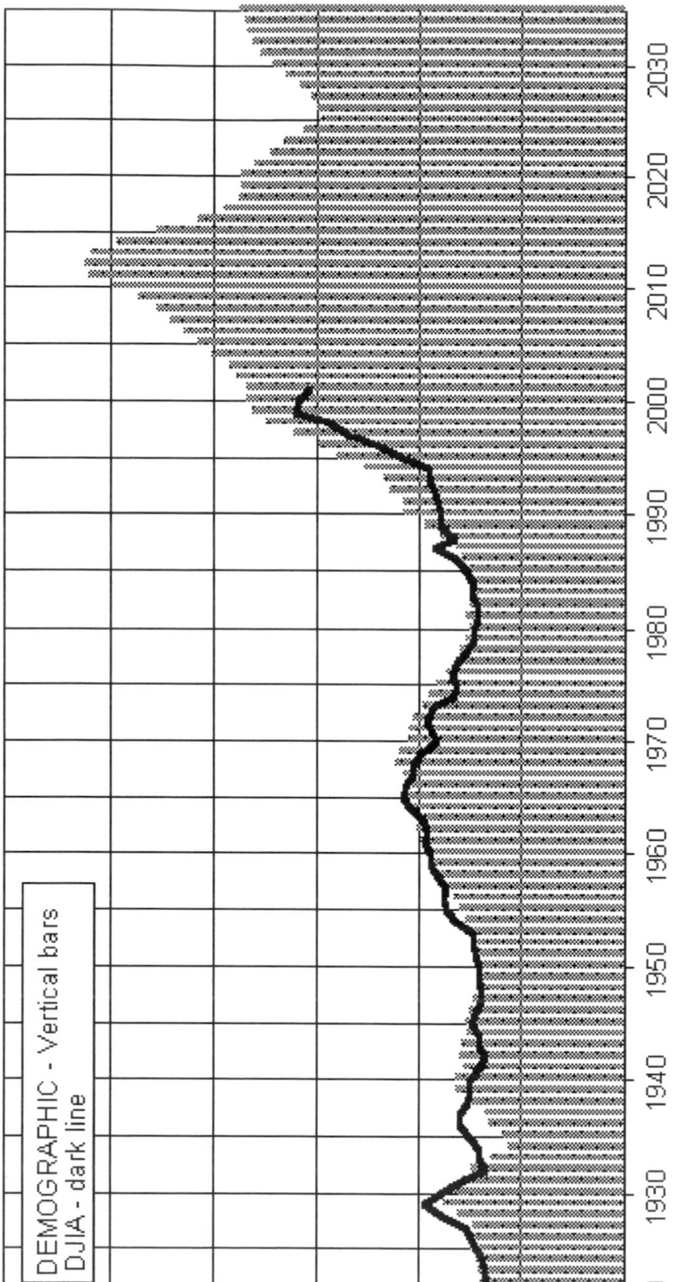

CHART 7 - DJIA vs "PILL CORRECTED" DEMOGRAPHIC PROFILE

DEMOGRAPHIC - Vertical bars
DJIA - dark line

away from bonds depressing bond prices. As a result, DJIA stocks although surging, were in fact being depressed by Nasdaq. While Nasdaq **was** very clearly full of "irrational exuberance", the DJIA clearly was **not**.

Folks, we are almost there. Let's take a quick look at the same curve, but using the simpler approach of only a single age of forty-nine years that was mentioned earlier. Take a look at Chart 8. Impressive, but clearly not usable as proof to validate a concept *beyond any doubt*. Now look at Chart 7 again. This is the moment to realize how breathtaking this chart is. You are looking at a chart that very accurately predicted the trend of the US economy for the best part of a century. For basic, simple, logical, easy to understand compelling reasons, it very closely follows the five-year age groupings of the highest spending people within the population at all times. The following conclusion is inevitable:

Eighty two years of tight correlation from 1920-2002 of the number of 45-54 year olds with the DJIA ups/downs (economy booms and busts) cannot possibly be a mere 82 year coincidence. That these big-spending Americans control the long-term peaks and valleys of the economy (the booms and busts), is now clearly beyond dispute. It really is as straightforward as that. The demographic model is correct.

CHART 8 - 49YR OLDS ONLY - INCLUDES IMMIGRATION

Demographic - Vertical bars
DJIA - dark line

18

All the reasons for the correlation have been explained and they are uncomplicated. In fact I would suggest that, once revealed, they are almost just plain commonsense.

But read on. The correlation only gets better and more incredible.

Picture this:

The great American economy is an ocean whose total depth is overwhelmingly made up of the combined spending of all the various age groups. The heaving waves on the surface of this deep ocean are always the "big spending" of the 45 to 54 year old group. These waves produce the peaks and troughs of the economy - the long-term booms and busts. Historically, as you have seen, they can and have both "raised and sunk ships". We will soon have to man the lifeboats as the monstrous, greatest demographic wave of 45-54 year olds in American history crashes down with a thunderous roar!

Like the great Titanic, there will not be enough time or enough lifeboats onboard, and only very limited rescue available.

Chapter 3   ALL THE MAJOR ECONOMIC EVENTS OF THE LAST EIGHTY YEARS EXPLAINED

Take a close look at Chart 7. You have probably already noticed that the DJIA is depressed from the demographic curve in two key places: 1939 to 1945, and 1966 to 1975. No prizes for this one. It is the Second World and Vietnam Wars. But notice the detail. The curve is not just approximately right. It is correct right down to the beginning dates and the end dates "snap-back" to the demographic. The obvious question is why doesn't the 1950 to 1953 Korean War show? The answer is clearly visible in Chart 7. The Korean War was in a period of economic (demographic) growth, while the Second World and Vietnam Wars were in periods of significant economic (demographic) decline. The impact of the Korean War on the consumer driven booming economy of the post war years was easily absorbed.

Now look at the correction on the DJIA in 1987. The so-called "crash of 1987." All that was happening was the DJIA getting ahead of itself after the clearly visible back to back rolling recessions of the 1970s. The DJIA simply snapped back to where it should have been and promptly carried on tracking the demographic again. As we now know, it was simply a brief, painful correction, *not* a crash.

Now look at the curve at the year 2000 point. The demographic curve clearly predicted a flattening of the economy lasting two or three years. That is exactly what is happening as I write this. And sure enough, look at the DJIA curve following the demographic reflecting the nagging mini-recession we've been in since 2000. Looking at Chart 7, is there any doubt in your mind that the DJIA will very shortly resume following the demographic, turning up by 2003 and rising all the way out to perhaps as far as 2012.

Now turn to the last major event on the chart. The crash of 1929 and the 1930s depression. Again, the demographic curve is spot-on right to the year. It clearly predicted the crash if anyone had known this relationship at the time. But why did the DJIA bottom in 1932 instead of following the demographic down to 1934? Again the answer is simple. After his election, President Roosevelt created the "New Deal" in 1933. Many massive public works programs were begun, such as roads, TVA, the Golden Gate and Bay Bridges and the Hoover Dam. It boosted the economy in the primarily manual labor environment of the time. In time of course the DJIA was forced back to the demographic line just as the Second World War began.

It is important to understand that markets crashing do not cause depressions or recessions. It is the other way around. The economy is simply following the demographic and declining. The DJIA then in turn reflects this in the value of stocks and itself declines. Sometimes the decline is steep and we call it a "crash." There is however something special however about the 1929 crash and 1930s depression. As you will recall, I said in Chapter 2 to remember the huge immigration of the early 1900s? Well, go back and look at Chart 4 again. Notice the huge immigration surge from 1900 to 1915. With an average age of around thirty, these hard-working immigrants showed up as middle-aged big spenders twenty years later in 1920 to 1935. They affected the demographic curve in a big way. Take a look at Chart 9. It is Chart 7 (1920 to 1960 only), but with immigration removed. Without the huge immigration, the demographic would have been a nice smooth rise all the way to 1960. This in turn would have given a steady growth in the economy all the way. No 1929 crash, no 1930s depression. High immigration from 1900 to 1915 is the fundamental, underlying reason for the roaring twenties, the crash of 1929 and the depression of the 1930s. Only this major economic event period, and one other described in the next chapter, have been significantly affected by immigration.

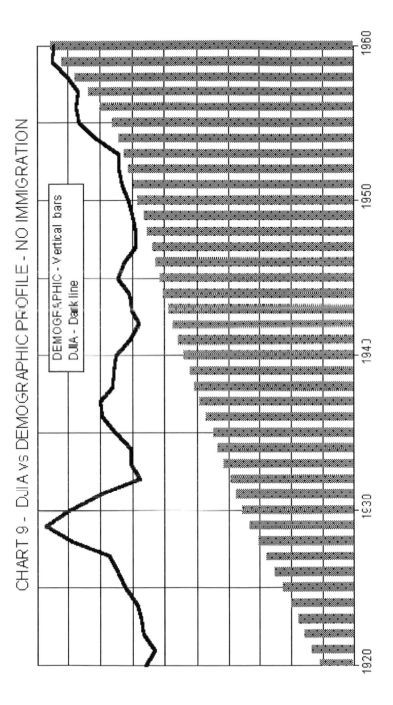

CHART 9 - DJIA vs DEMOGRAPHIC PROFILE - NO IMMIGRATION

DEMOGRAPHIC - Vertical bars
DJIA - Dark line

1920   1930   1940   1950   1960

23

Chapter 4   THE FUTURE - 2003 to 2025

By looking at Chart 7 I think it is now obvious to you that the USA is on the verge of a maximum of a decade of solid economic growth and a steady rise in the DJIA. After that, starting **no later than 2012-13**, an economic decline of terrible proportions begins and lasts until about 2025. Now you understand why the baby-boomers are not going to have a pleasant retirement. I said earlier on that there are in fact 100 million baby-boomers (not the much lower number of about 75 million you hear quoted). They are the huge demographic ramp-up shown in Chart 7 starting about 1986 and going to 2012. When backed off to their birth years we get 1936 to 1962. If you add up these births, which includes immigrant boomers, it is over a 100 million. Traditionally, the baby boomers are identified as those born starting arbitrarily in 1946. Economically this is very incorrect.

Now in Chart 7 compare the drop in the demographic curve in the 1930-35 period to the monstrous drop coming in 2013-2025. I will quantify its impact shortly. Fasten your seat belt!

2003 to 2012

Starting sometime in the latter half of 2002 or in 2003, the economy will resume its march upwards accompanied by the matching rise in the DJIA. The peak it rises to, which I will also easily quantify shortly, is the other major economic event that is affected by immigration. Go back and look at Chart 4 again. You will notice a huge surge in legal immigration from 1989 to 1993. It totals an incredible 6.3 million! With their average age of around 30, they will show up as big spending fifty-year olds in 2009 to 2013, right when the demographic without them will be peaking anyway. They will just drive it to new heights and amplify the subsequent peak from which the economy and DJIA will fall.

So, the next ten years represents the last chance for a very long time to make any money by traditionally investing in stocks. There is a big caveat though. The returns are not going to be anything like the 1990s. Why would this be? The slope of the demographic curve looks almost as steep as the 1990s. It is, but let me explain it this way. Imagine the demographic curve from 1992 to 2012 is a 20 foot ladder and you are now standing about half way up at the year 2002. When you were standing on the first rung in 1992 you were one foot above the ground. You are now 10 feet off the ground (2002). Your height increased a whopping 900%. When you go from the tenth rung that you are on (2002) to the top 20 foot rung (2012), you will only increase your height from 10 feet to 20 feet, a mere 100%. In other words the big returns were on the early rungs of the ladder in the 1990s. The second half of the rungs is going to give modest returns even though the slope is very similar.

What will those returns be? The first step is to project where the DJIA is going. Take a look at Chart 10. I have marked a very *conservative* path for the DJIA through 2030. Now that you know what is really going on, you could do it just as easily as I have. In the Vorago database that produces these curves it is high school arithmetic to convert any projected DJIA path to actual DJIA numbers. The projected DJIA path of Chart 10 peaks at about 26,000. A path chosen to follow the demographic tightly would peak at about 32,000. Regardless of the path used, the percentage magnitude of the subsequent decline from 2013 to year 2025 hardly changes.

Remember, all this is not the guessed at "opinion" of a TV analyst (who never gives you this kind of information). This is simply the result of recognizing that the DJIA has very tightly and relentlessly followed the demographic driver for over 80 years for fundamental, understandable reasons, and that it is inevitably going to continue to do so. If the Second World and Vietnam Wars only sideswiped the DJIA slightly, it is hard to imagine what events can possibly prevent

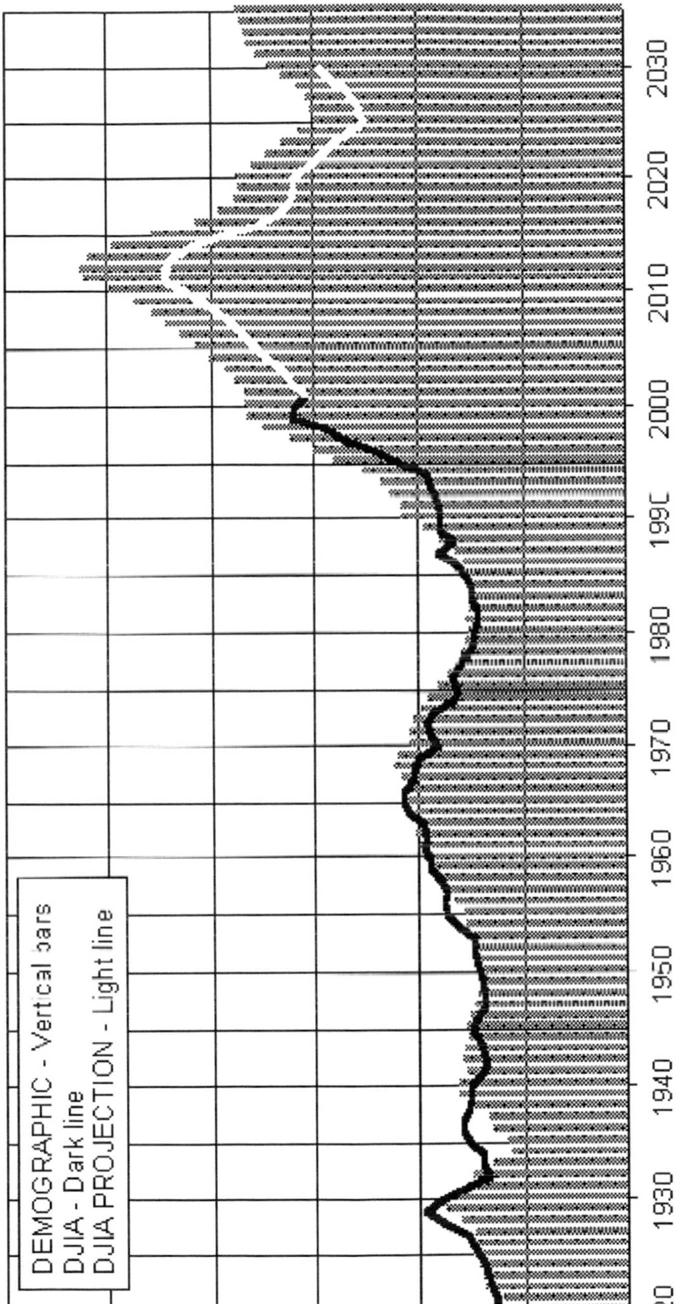

CHART 10 - DJIA w PROJECTION vs DEMOGRAPHIC PROFILE

DEMOGRAPHIC - Vertical bars
DJIA - Dark line
DJIA PROJECTION - Light line

the future from being a tracking repeat of the past eighty years. *The long-term trajectory of the economy and DJIA is now clearly seen to always be predetermined by our demographics.* Not its exact peak value each year, but the primary path that it will be forced to follow over a period of years. Arithmetically, inflation does affect the peak and valley DJIA numbers in the database, but does not change the magnitude of what is coming in any significant way. Again, simple arithmetic enables the DJIA peak to be forecast for each year into the future. This in turn enables the annual returns to be simply determined. Take a look at Chart 11 to see the modest, historically normal 7% to 8% average return for 2003 through 2012. The analysts have got this one right. They regularly now warn only to expect historically normal returns in the future years. They do it for the wrong reason though. They say it just because we can't "expect" the high double digit returns of the 1990s. The one piece of bright news is that, as Chart 10 shows, the DJIA has been driven too low in the current decline by the Nasdaq bubble bursting and corporate scandals. *The DJIA snap back to the demographic line that must happen in 2003/2004, will be to about 13,000 to 14,000 at least, and the FTSE in the UK to 6,000 to 7,000. It is a one-time opportunity. Do your best not to miss it!* If Chart 11 or

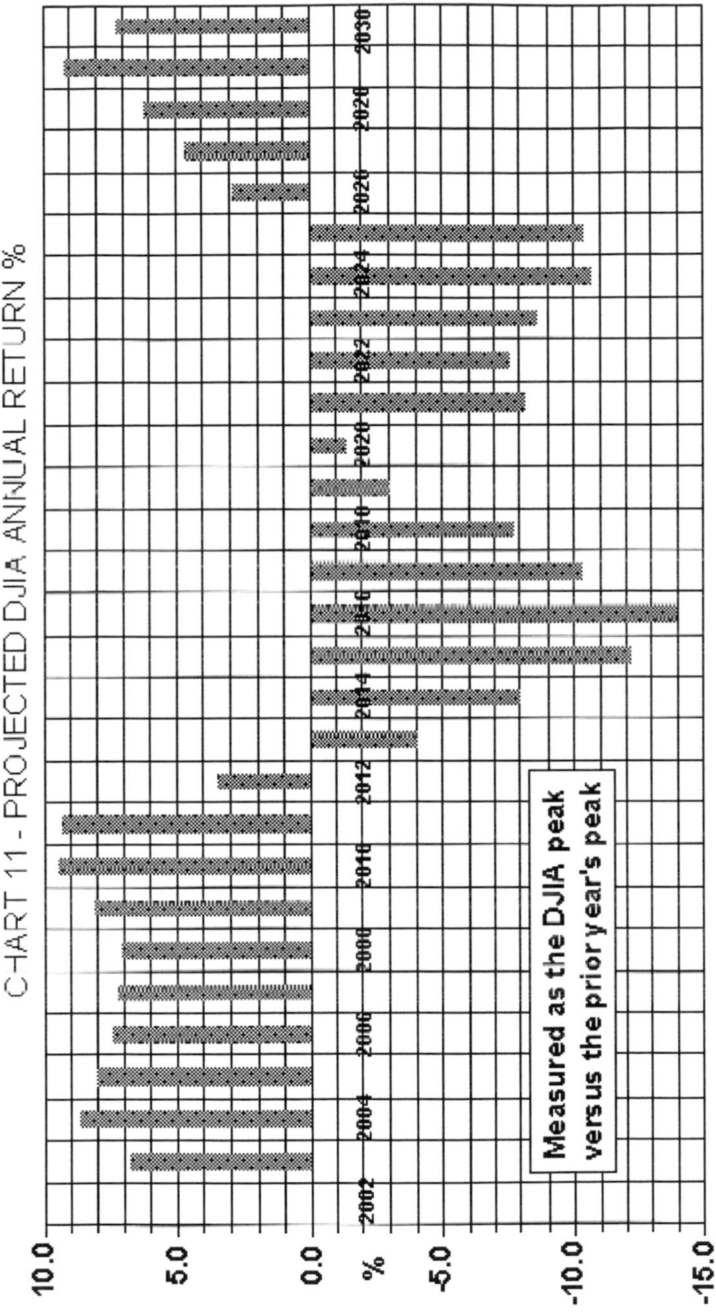

CHART 11 - PROJECTED DJIA ANNUAL RETURN %

Measured as the DJIA peak versus the prior year's peak

29

the snap-back turn out not to be correct for a specific year, don't get too upset. Remember, the entire concept of this book is directed at *long-term* trends, *not* each year. Any specific year can be at great variance with Chart 11 due to wars, politics, terrorism and scandals etc. So, don't throw the baby out with the bath water if this happens. Never forget that **history shows that the DJIA curve always rejoins the demographic line over time**, and for good reasons that you now understand. Also, take note that Chart 11 measures the yearly returns based on the DJIA peak versus the prior year's peak, not the somewhat meaningless lows.

Isn't it ironic that the analysts are always trying to forecast the short-term economy, which is an impossible task. The long-term, which you now know is very predictable, is never talked about - **and that's where the real danger now lies for us all** - people, businesses, institutions and nations.

2013 to 2025

The show is over, well and truly over. No amount of stimulation or other form of economic mouth-to-mouth is going to make a bit of difference. As you will recall, I showed you in Chapter 2 how you and I *are* the economy. As Chart 10 shows, from 2013 to 2025 the big-spending 45 to 54 year olds among us are only there in relentlessly declining numbers. Those we will have at any given time were always made 45 to 54 years before. It is almost sad to think that the baby-boomers' retirement years were economically set in concrete half a century ago.

Just how big is this catastrophic depression going to be financially? In the stock market crash from 1929 to 1932, the value of stocks dropped approximately $90 billion. When expressed in year 2000 dollars and adjusted to match the size of the population now versus then (284M vs 123M), this is a drop of about **2.6 TRILLION dollars**. It directly affected the less than five percent of the population who owned stocks at the time. The population at large was affected by job loss and the ensuing poverty. When the 2013 to 2025 decline of the DJIA, shown in Chart 10, is converted with simple arithmetic to the loss in the value of all stocks in the same year 2000 dollars, it is a staggering **18 TRILLION dollars. This is seven times as bad as 1929 to 1932 - and this is based on a conservative path in chart 10!** The actual loss in dollars of the time will be more like $24 Trillion. This is all bad enough, but there is a terrible difference this time. This time the loss directly affects the more than fifty percent of us that now own stocks either directly, or in mutual funds, pension plans, IRA or 401K type plans (ISAs and TESSAs etc. in the UK). It will be a financial holocaust. This of course will be just the beginning. In the depths of the depression of the 1930s, when the GDP dropped by a whopping 50%, both US and UK unemployment reached 25%. With a depression that is financially about seven times as deep as the 1930s, what will unemployment reach this time? As in the 1930s, home values will also plummet destroying much of the homeowner's equity, or all of it for those who buy homes in the years leading up to 2012-13.

So there it is. Now you know. Don't let anyone tell you it is not going to happen. I know of no alternate scenario being put forth that successfully covers the one hundred and six years (1920-2025 inclusive) that this book covers. If there is, I would like to see it defended against the hard facts of this book.

This catastrophic depression will happen whether the government tells us about it or not. Use this book to help plan your long-term future as best you can. Imagine it is 1922 and you know with certainty that the crash of 1929-32 and the depression of the 1930s are coming. What will you do? You must use the precious few years that are left to prepare. It still won't be enough time for many or perhaps most, but at least forewarned is forearmed.

SUMMARY

The ups and downs (booms and busts) of the long-term economy are clearly proven to be controlled by the demographic of how many big-spending 45 to 54 year olds there are in the population at any given time. The economy, as reflected by the inflation adjusted DJIA, has tightly followed this demographic for the best part of the last one hundred years. The correlation, when five-year age groupings are used, is so stunning that every major economic event of the century can be accounted for simply and accurately. The statistical probability that this relationship exists for about a century by sheer chance is minuscule. Because we reliably know this demographic decades into the future at all times, the long-term path of the economy is very predictable and easily measurable.

This demographic shows us that solid economic growth with modest stock market returns will occur from 2003 onward, but then around 2012-2013 latest, a depression that is of an historically unprecedented magnitude begins and lasts until around 2025. It's shocking financial magnitude in year 2000 dollars (for a valid comparison) is about seven times greater than the crash of 1929-1932. The full domestic and international impacts may be so severe as to be unpredictable in scope.

IMPORTANT: Remember, it's <u>not</u> the Baby Boomers retiring that is going to collapse the economy. As Chart 7 shows, it's the catastrophic decline in the number of big-spending, "GDP driving" 45-54 year old Boomers that is the problem. This is 11-20 years <u>before</u> their retirement.

Chapter 5   DON'T LISTEN TO THE ECONOMISTS

As we approach 2013 it is very important to *not* listen to traditional economists regarding the long-term economy, if they should ever try to talk about it. Why? Apart from quite literally threatening your long-term health, their track record for a century was, and still is, absolutely miserable:

Traditional economists as a group failed to forecast ALL the major events:

- The 1929-32 stock market crash
- The 1930s depression
- The 14 years of rolling recessions from 1968-1982
- The "crash" (correction) of 1987
- The massive boom of the 1990s
- The 2000 to 2002+ severe decline of the stock markets

   . . . . AND NOW,

- The coming historically unprecedented depression of ~2013 to 2025

Many times over the last several years I said to myself "but surely, surely *they* must know all this", *"they"* being the large cadre of distinguished establishment professionals. Perhaps they do, but if they do they are sure being awfully quiet about it, and it's certainly not doing the nation a service to be quiet about it if they do know. Clearly, a case can be made for being quiet about it for political reasons, but that's politicians and not the financial/economics community. Or, perhaps they don't know, or more to the point, they don't want to know. History shows clearly that the gurus only very reluctantly move away from status quo ideas on "how things work" to embrace new (demographics) information, even when the new facts scream loudly and explain our economic history beautifully. Consider the following as you think about it:

On January 23rd 1987 on the Wall Street Week TV program, Alan Greenspan declared ***"The American economy will decline in the 1990s."*** The 1990s were the greatest boom in history, and easy to so predict using the uncomplicated data in this book. What on earth was the data Alan Greenspan was looking at? Whatever it was, or whatever economic theory he subscribed to, it was absolutely, totally wrong. He is now installed as the USA's top economist as chairman of the Federal Reserve. What more needs to be said? We listen to them at our peril.

The following chapter deals with what you *can* do as individuals. Others must take the critical data of this book and convert it into recommendations for business, institutions, politicians and diplomats.

Chapter 6   WHAT ON EARTH CAN YOU DO?

If you are not asking this question by now it is either because you're still in shock, or you don't believe any of it. If it is the latter, you may very well stand to lose much of your net worth, be it large or small. How anyone, faced with the stark facts I have presented, cannot believe that the future laid out above is really going to happen, is a little hard to understand. It would be a bit like that poor fellow who was running his lodge up at Spirit Lake and refused to believe that Mount St. Helens, even if it blew, presented any real danger. We all know what happened. Those who can overcome the natural reaction of denying to themselves that this could possibly happen to their generation, will stand the best chance of surviving the coming catastrophic depression and even doing quite well throughout. Those that put their head in the sand or worse, believe the fairy tale idea that *"the government doesn't let that kind of thing happen anymore"*, will be big losers. ***The government has absolutely no power to stop it - repeat, absolutely none! Did they stop 2000-2002?***

There *are* definite things you can do. You must save and invest as much as you can while the last of the stock market sun is still shining. This is the calm before the storm. You must take full advantage of the last few years of the baby-boomer driven growth economy between now and 2012. Stocks are the place to be, but you must not get too close to the edge. The easiest play is to invest in an S&P 500 Index Fund offered by many institutions such as Vanguard and Invesco/AIM. If you are not a sophisticated investor with time to spend studying and investing in individual stocks, this is a good approach. Over time very, very few mutual funds have beaten this index. It's simple. It works. But, get 100% of your savings and pension moneys out of stocks and stock based investments (such as mutual funds in the US and unit trusts in the UK), by 2010 at the very latest. This may leave money on the table, but it's better to play it safe as the precipice looms. This will definitely not be the time for brinkmanship. Even 2010 may be cutting it close. If you can, roll your 401K into your IRA (without penalty) where it will be under your direct control and invested as you decide. This will ensure it does not become a victim of the future "financial condition" of the employer or company the 401K is with. An independent financial advisor can help you, especially if the 401K administrator resists. Get as much as possible under your control.

There may be some substantial market ups and downs along the way to 2012. The temporary effects of a "911", war, corporate scandals and other unforeseen events cannot be removed. Remember, all the facts presented in this book are *long-term* trend related. In the short-term (one to three years), anything can happen. The depression may begin as early as 2010 or even 2009. You should share all this with your cross-generational adult family and, as time goes by, with your teenage children especially. They may be looking at going to college and then finding jobs in a depression of catastrophic proportions. They need to understand what lies ahead for them and prepare themselves too.

So, where could you go with your money once you are out of stocks? This is an easy one. In times of economic depression interest rates always fall. They have to. Few want to risk borrowing money to buy houses, build businesses or invest in whatever. Money is just a commodity and, as demand for it falls, its price (interest rate) drops, just like prices for TVs, cars or hotel rooms. So, the place to consider for your savings and pension monies is bonds - intermediate and long-term bonds. Why bonds? As interest rates fall, the value of existing bonds goes up because the higher interest rate it is paying to its owner makes it more valuable in the eyes of others. As a rule of thumb, if interest rates drop in half, a long bond's value will double. You must obviously get into bonds before interest rates drop. This means *before* the crash.

Only go for the best quality. This means federal government bonds. There is a very real risk, perhaps even a certainty, that corporate and state issued bonds will default in this depression. Stay with Uncle Sam. You can buy bonds directly or through a brokerage service, or simply buy a long or medium term Treasury Bond mutual fund. For simplicity, or if you don't have a lot to invest, use a large mutual fund group like Vanguard or Fidelity. *Make sure you also carefully read the real estate section in Chapter 7.*

If you think of social security as *your* money, as you should, can you now see why putting some of it into the stock market in the coming years to improve your ultimate benefits, as some members of congress are advocating, is a folly of truly monumental proportion? Sophisticated, savvy investors may very well stand to benefit, but the average person will not. They will simply become victims of the equity markets, which now include a coming unprecedented depression. It will be lambs to the financial slaughter.

The following chapters deal at a very top level with the catastrophic social, business and international consequences. Experts in these areas must predict what will happen in detail during such a terrible depression. A final chapter deals with the Vorago database.

Chapter 7   THE SOCIAL IMPACT

<u>Unemployment</u>

In the 1930s depression, unemployment peaked at 25% in both the USA and the UK. In the USA 13 million were unemployed. It is difficult to predict, but with the numbers you have seen showing that the financial depth of the coming depression is seven times greater than the 1930s, it seems a very safe assumption that we will again see at least 25%. ***This translates to at least 30 million out of work***. It is a rate that we can barely contemplate in terms of what it will be like. Let me put this in shocking perspective - numerically this is the equivalent of every single worker in a country the size of Germany being 100% unemployed. Rates of just 10% send shock waves through our society today. Those that were twenty in 1932 are now 90 or dead. There are very few left to articulate those days to us. Old films and news clips can only go so far. Can you imagine desperate war veterans camped outside the White House by the thousands, demanding money *promised* to them by the US government? That's just one example of what happened in the 1930s. They were eventually tear-gassed and their camps burned. They got nothing.

There will be unemployment benefits, but they will only last a few months, and will in no way be the solution for anyone. It will be like trying to cross the desert with only a pint of water. There will be thirteen years of financial desert to cross. With so many unemployed it is very doubtful whether benefits will be totally payable.

Huge declines in city services

Towns and cities are very heavily dependent upon their property and sales tax bases to fund their activities, along with the various state and federal tax distributions. Every single one of these tax bases will shrink dramatically. As unemployment grips the society, declines in spending will shrink the sales tax base. As real estate foreclosures snowball, the property tax base will shrink. If the property tax is indexed to property values, the tax base will shrink further as the value of all types of property plummets. With growing unemployment, state and federal income tax revenues will inevitably decline causing allocations to cities to be reduced.

Just like companies on hard times, cities will be forced to lay workers off, contributing further to unemployment. As cities lay off, whatever services those employees provided will be reduced. The first wave of layoffs will get the fat. The second and subsequent waves will hit muscle - the police and fire departments, sanitation and social services.

City services we take for granted today will be less and less available.

Huge increase in crime

Higher and higher unemployment will breed higher and higher crime rates as desperate people, particularly poorer, unskilled young men, turn to crime to survive. The reduced police services will mean the tidal wave of crime will be less and less manageable. With the number of hand guns now in circulation at epidemic levels, an especially dangerous edge will be given to this crime wave. More crime will inevitably generate far more prosecutions and prison terms. The prisons, which are already maxed out today, will also be suffering from reduced funding, just like everything else as the tax bases shrink.

Huge income tax increases

As the state and federal governments run out of money, they have little option but to increase taxes, or in the case of the federal, print more money. The latter of course will just devalue the currency. In states where balancing the budget is mandated by law, the state must either cut services, or increase taxes, or raise money with bonds. The latter means going into debt just like you or I would. As always, they will vote to raise taxes. This will immediately give those still working even less money to spend. Retail businesses then see less sales and lay more people off. Laid off people pay no income taxes. They apply for benefits and thereby put more demand on the states which are getting less and less tax flowing into their coffers. *It is a spiraling vortex that feeds on itself. This is what depressions are made of*.

Private enterprise cannot provide jobs if it cannot turn a profit. So it is left to the government to do what it can. In the thirties it was the New Deal creating huge public works programs. Maybe this will be tried again to give some relief. Perhaps the interstate highways will get repaired at long last!

Healthcare and social security

It is important to remember that while all this devastation will be going on, something else very special is happening. The massive group of 100 million baby-boomers will be entering retirement and demanding their social security benefits promised to them all their lives. Let me put the baby-boomers into a shocking perspective for you:

The boomers as a group approach in size the entire population of Japan - every man woman and child! Think of it. Try to get your mind around the magnitude of it.

The very earliest "true" boomers (born in the mid 1930s), started to enter retirement in

2000. The first of the post-war "traditional" boomers enters in 2011. By 2015 it will be a flood that will not let up until about 2027. They will impact two main areas with full force - the social security and healthcare systems. The latter is comprised of private healthcare such as HMOs, and then the federal, state and locally funded hospitals, Medicare and Medicaid systems. The healthcare system will also be under progressively increasing pressure from the tens of millions of unemployed people as well as lower paid employed people, all seeking healthcare that they cannot pay for. There is the real prospect that the healthcare of much of the population will collapse to a third world standard.

Social security benefits is the one area that even today is already in the public arena for discussion. With the huge baby-boomer wave long ago seen to be moving toward retirement, scared bureaucrats have for years been planning the ongoing multi-trillion dollar trust fund that must support it. Yet there are still persistent fears that it is not secure. Fears that are very justified because the trust fund doesn't really exist. Any surplus after current pay-outs to existing retirees goes into the Treasury general fund for spending on anything the government wants. It's like a company pension plan that has nothing in it, just the company promising to pay you from company assets when due. The US government insists that social security is secure until 2030, but what level of Social Security tax revenues are they assuming for 2013 to 2025 to support pay-outs? I very seriously doubt they are using the dramatically slashed levels of revenue that will occur during a catastrophic thirteen year depression. Nothing remotely as big as this combination of a huge group of retired boomers and a catastrophic depression has ever happened historically. We are truly going where no one has gone before. We use the term *"boomers"* so glibly today without realizing they (we) are a ticking time bomb. The taxes of those left working during this coming depression have to support this benefits Goliath. It is a staggering task even without the healthcare challenge.

Businesses

As unemployment gets worse, wages will inevitably decline as competition for jobs becomes fierce beyond anything in living memory. This in turn generates even less in federal and state income tax revenues and of course even lower consumer spending. This in turn generates less sales tax, which of course in turn . . . . . you know the rest.

Slowly but surely, businesses will cut prices to survive. When price cutting and declining sales reach a critical point, small businesses (where most jobs in the economy are), that cannot make ends meet, will go out of business. The shopping malls, small town high street stores and small factories will progressively become more and more vacant. All the bank loans, large or small, extended to these businesses or commercial real estate corporations, will become bad loans. Loans made by banks that go bad are not insured by the government. As the bad loans from commercial ventures, large and small, and mounting foreclosures escalate, the likelihood of bank failures becomes a real possibility, especially when overseas loans default too. Most of the consumers' bank deposits are insured by the FDIC (Federal Deposit Insurance Corporation), but any such payout on this insurance has to be met by the government, and becomes another huge liability against dwindling reserves.

Real estate

Although we can become very emotionally attached to it, real estate is just a commodity. Prices for new property set the price for existing *used* property, as with cars for example. As the demand for new homes plummets, the price of existing homes will follow suit, just like in the 1930s. Those with 30% or less equity in their property will surely lose it all. Those with little or modest equity will quickly find their home is worth less than their mortgage. With this, and the loss of employment and income for so many homeowners, foreclosures will become an epidemic. However, for those who own a home with substantial equity, and have the stomach for it, there will be a great survival opportunity presented by the depression. As real estate prices peak toward the end of the economic upswing, perhaps no later than 2010, sell your home and rent. US federal tax laws permit couples to pocket up to $500,000 of capital gains on the sale of a home without paying tax on it. As described in chapter 6, put the proceeds into long-term federal treasury bonds. When the depression hits, your bonds will surge in value, plus you will then be able to buy a home for a song. For example, let's say your home can sell for $400,000 in 2010 and you bought it for $150,000 some years before, and you now owe perhaps $50,000 on the mortgage. Disregarding the costs of its sale, your cash in hand will be $350,000. Let's say you pocket $50,000 for living and put the balance of $300,000 into long term bonds which should be earning 5% to 6% by then (about $16,000 of steady income per year to offset income or job loss). I conservatively project 5% to 6%, as it is clear that from the very low inflation level and record low interest rates we are now at in 2002, we can only see some inflation in the next decade as the economy recovers and continues to grow again. This will push interest rates up.

When the depression hits and long-term interest rates perhaps drop in half, your bonds will surge in value to around $600,000. You can now buy a home like you had before for perhaps $280,000. In this example you will end up $320,000 ahead of the game plus the bonds interest income you received. This will be offset by capital gains tax on the bonds' growth as you sell them, home selling costs, whatever rents you have paid, and tax benefits from home ownership you gave up during this time. You should do the math for your own particular situation to assess your specific opportunity. It will take courage to do this move.

The International impact

The American economy is so massive it always affects the entire world's economy in a huge way. What happens economically in the USA determines in part what life is like in much of the industrialized world and beyond. The more any country is dependent upon the American economy the worse will be the impact on them. The most dependent is Mexico. Many of the fully industrialized nations of Chart 1 (except Japan), have similar demographics to the USA. They will also undergo a "middle-aged" demographic downturn just like the USA. They will also be experiencing the economic impact of lost trade with the USA during the depression. Japan, as we know, has a very large aged population at this time. Japan's "boomers", or whatever we might call them, clearly entered retirement one or two decades ago and probably drove Japan's economy into the severe recession it has been in since 1990.

---------- 2006 JAPAN UPDATE ----------

The data is now in that clearly shows that the 13 year severe recession in Japan from 1990 to 2003 was caused by a decline in their "big spenders" demographic wave just as our coming depression will be. Look at Chart 12. It shows the Japanese 39-43 years old demographic versus the inflation-adjusted Nikkei. The demographic plunged from 1990 to 2003 and the Japanese economy followed it all the way down to 2003. In 2003 the demographic turned up and the Nikkei has faithfully followed it up ever since. The obvious question is "why are the Japanese big-spenders centered on about 41 years old compared to America's about 50 years old?"
Per Japan's Ministry of Labor, peak earnings occur at 40 years old at smaller companies and 50 years old at large corporations. This phenomenon is the result of what is called the "seniority-based wage system" in Japan. As in America, the vast majority of jobs are in small companies, driving their peak spending

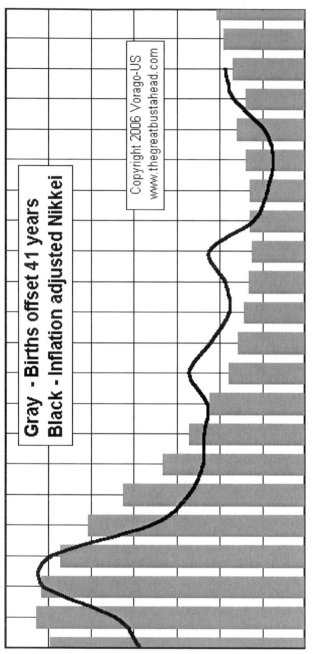

CHART 12 - JAPAN 39-43 YR OLDS DEMOGRAPHIC vs NIKKEI

Gray - Births offset 41 years
Black - Inflation adjusted Nikkei

Copyright 2006 Vorago-US
www.thegreatbustahead.com

1987 1988 1989 1990 1991 1992 1993 1994 1995 1996 1997 1998 1999 2000 2001 2002 2003 2004 2005 2006 2007

years lower and towards 40. Don't forget that Japan has been kept afloat during its severe 1990-2003 recession by feeding on the booming USA and European economies. As a big exporting nation, this kept Japan from being in a true depression. When America goes into depression, it is very unlikely to have any other booming economies to export to that will help keep America afloat. On the contrary, the great dependence others have on the American economy (e.g. Mexico and Canada), will drive them into depression too.

The USA is a net importer of goods. As this dries up, the "exporting to the USA nations of the world" including China, will feel the pinch big time. As the American economy shrinks (Note: the GDP in the 1930s shrank 50%), our demand for oil for example, will plummet. In 2002 it is currently about $27 a barrel. It is very likely that oil will fall below $5 a barrel (which will help us to a degree). This seems unthinkable today, especially to oil exporting nations for sure. But oil is just a commodity with its price ultimately set by demand. All of us have to learn to think in "never before experienced" catastrophic depression terms.

As our ability as a nation to make ends meet gets worse, our wherewithal to extend help to other nations will be heavily compromised. Only politicians and diplomats can know what we should do in such a highly complex and sensitive situation. Withdrawing or limiting foreign aid has important ramifications that affect our national security and the stability of nations. It also affects the very basic fabric of third world countries where declining American aid and trade may bring abject poverty and even starvation. No matter what happens in the area of American foreign aid, the third world is going to suffer terribly.

Such deteriorating third world conditions breed something else - turmoil. As things worsen, voices proclaiming "this is what free enterprise leads to, especially *American* free enterprise" will be more and more listened to, just as they were in the 1930s. They will find eager ears in the third world. This kind of desperate and deteriorating environment is what helped despots of the first half of the twentieth century to come to power. It is a very complex area that industrialized nation governments must find ways to deal with in order to bring the world out of this coming depression intact, if that is in fact possible.

What can you do for your country?

- Oppose the crazy partial investment of our social security money in the stock market.
- Support programs that seem to give the healthcare system at large a better chance of surviving very hard times with the unprecedented two pressures of

100,000,000+ retiring baby-boomers and huge numbers of poor and unemployed.

- Support initiatives and those politicians that push to increase our exports. The more we export the more we can make our economy dependent on people other than our big-spending 45 to 54 year olds.

- Oppose pork barrel programs everywhere. Don't vote for candidates with pork barrel histories. Our government needs to spend our money on things that will truly help us in the coming depression

- Even if you would not support gun-control in economically healthy times, consider supporting gun control legislation to help take the dangerous edge off the crime wave that will hit during the depression.

- Regardless of your political persuasion, carefully consider when casting your ballot both locally and nationally, which party's policies will be the best to help our nation (and the world) during the terrible times ahead. Be flexible. It will certainly not be a time to vote out of habit.

- Give a copy of this low cost book to every branch of your family before it is too late.

- Refer friends and colleagues to the book's website: **www.thegreatbustahead.com** The more that get to understand what is coming the better.

You are going to spend about 25% of your adult life in this terrible depression. Just think about it - 25%! This is serious stuff.

Finally, don't make the *"It's the Boomers retiring"* mistake. Let me remind you again:

It's <u>not</u> the Baby Boomers retiring that is going to collapse the economy. As shown in Chart 7, it's the catastrophic decline in the number of "big-spending, GDP driving" 45-54 year old Boomers that is the problem. This is 11 to 20 years <u>before</u> their retirement.

Their retirement does however <u>very</u> greatly worsen the funding problems with Social Security and Medicare. In the worse case it may even essentially destroy them, or at least dramatically change them from what they have been in the past.

A brief word on China and India: as you have seen, the economies of fully industrialized democracies (which they are not) are ***driven overwhelmingly by the spending of their consumers. When our inevitable "low spending" demographic abyss arrives the depression begins regardless***. What China and India do just doesn't matter, except that their competition for oil and low prices make our situation worse. They cannot afford to buy much of what we make because our products are just too expensive due to production costs, primarily labor and benefits.

Chapter 8   THE VORAGO DATABASE

The engine behind all the analysis that has culminated in the revelations and warnings of this book is the Vorago database. Vorago is Latin for "Abyss" reflecting the economic journey we will all be undertaking from about 2013 to 2025, and perhaps as early as 2009.

This chapter is intended to give those so inclined, an insight into the structure of the database, and how it can be used on an ongoing basis by those who wish to consider purchasing this proprietary database. The user-friendly version of the Vorago database runs on Microsoft Excel version 7.0 and later.

The Vorago database's user-friendly data entry and output permit easy and rapid entry of the following data. The resulting output screen allows exploration of multiple results using these wide ranging inputs:

ENTRY 1

- Five-year age groupings of choice (45-49 years to 51-55 years) for 1920 to 2035.

ENTRY 2

- Projected Consumer Price Index inflation rate (CPI) from the current year to 2030.
- Actual DJIA yearly highs as they occur, from the current year onwards.

ENTRY 3

- A curve shaping multiplier that enables the best vertical positioning of the DJIA versus the Demographics curves in the charts. The data itself is in no way affected.

ENTRY 4

- A tracking factor (0 to 1), for how close the projected future DJIA should track the future demographic. A "1" would be exact glove fit tracking. This determines the path the DJIA will follow and the peak reached.

ENTRY 5

- The percentage of immigrants to be factored into the demographics.

ENTRY 6

- The projected number of immigrants for each future year out to 2016.

The core data is the fixed demographics of the American population from 1870 to today, and the overwhelmingly fixed demographics (as far as big-spending 45 to 54 year olds are concerned) from today to 2035, along with the following non-demographic fixed data:

- The US census derived data 1870 to 1909 relating to birth rates and total population, tabulated by decade. The very linear results permit reliable extrapolation to create yearly data. From these two, the births per year are estimated for 1870 through 1909.

- Annual births from 1910 (when the government records began) onwards are used until the present.

- Annual immigration from government records from 1870 until the present, tabulated by year.

- Annual inflation rates as expressed by the CPI from 1920 to present.

- The historical annual highs of the DJIA as determined from the daily closing highs. A separate section of the Vorago database stores the daily closings for the DJIA for every day from 1920 to 2001.

Straightforward algorithms permit the combination of the "historically fixed" data with "variable" Inputs 1 through 6 to create most of the charts in this book, and more.

For reference, a default data entry set for entries 1 through 6 that generated most of the charts of this book, is included as part of the user-friendly version of the database.

****

Those interested in purchasing the user-friendly version of the Vorago database should make e-mail contact through the website at: www.thegreatbustahead.com

INDEX